FOR ORGANS, PIANOS & ELECTRONIC KEYBOARDS

74

Over the Rainbow
& 40 MORE GREAT SONGS

ISBN 978-1-4950-2608-9

HAL•LEONARD®
CORPORATION

7777 W. BLUEMOUND RD. P.O. BOX 13819 MILWAUKEE, WI 53213

Visit Hal Leonard Online at
www.halleonard.com

At Last

Registration 3
Rhythm: Ballad or Swing

Lyric by Mack Gordon
Music by Harry Warren

Cute

Registration 7
Rhythm: Swing or Fox Trot

Music by Neal Hefti
Words by Stanley Styne

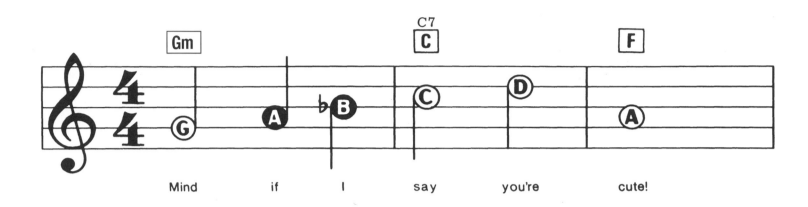

Mind if I say you're cute!

In ev - 'ry way you're

cute! Those big blue

eyes, That turned - up nose,

Feeling Good

from THE ROAR OF THE GREASEPAINT – THE SMELL OF THE CROWD

Registration 8
Rhythm: 4/4 Ballad or Rock

Words and Music by Leslie Bricusse
and Anthony Newley

Bird fly - ing high, you know how I feel.
Fish in the sea, you know how I feel.

Sun in the sky, you know how I feel. Breeze drift - ing by,
Riv - er run - ning free, you know how I feel. Blos - som on the tree,

you know how I feel.
you know how I feel.} It's a new dawn, it's a new day, it's a

new life ____ for ____ me, ____ feel - ing good. ____

Good Morning Starshine
from the Broadway Musical Production HAIR

Registration 4
Rhythm: Rock

Words by James Rado
and Gerome Ragni
Music by Galt MacDermot

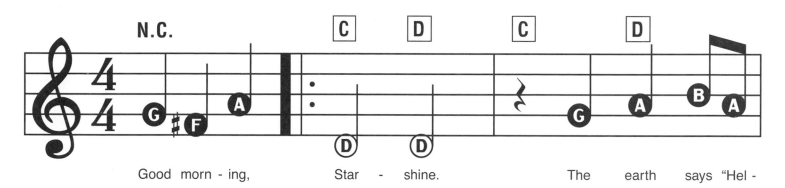

Good morn - ing, Star - shine. The earth says "Hel -

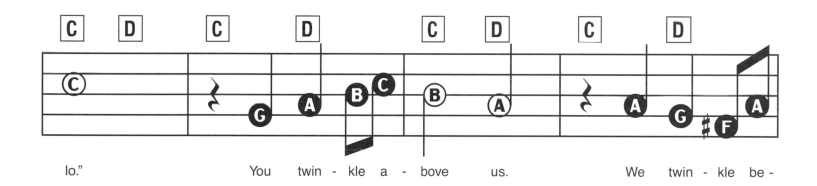

lo." You twin - kle a - bove us. We twin - kle be -

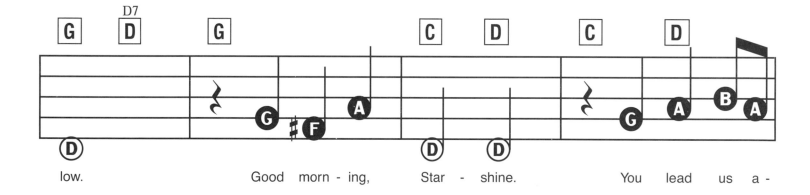

low. Good morn - ing, Star - shine. You lead us a -

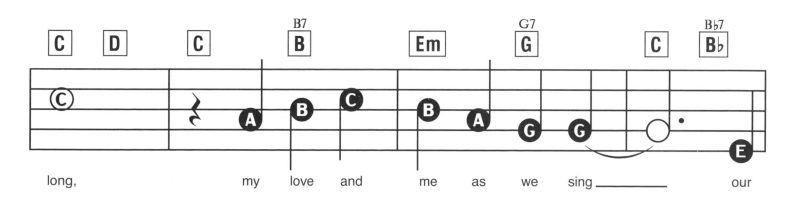

long, my love and me as we sing _____ our

13

Gentle Rain

Registration 4
Rhythm: Bossa Nova or Latin

Music by Luiz Bonfa
Words by Matt Dubey

D.C. al Coda
(Return to beginning
Play to ⊕ and
Skip to Coda)

will be your love for a while. _____
love will be sweet, will be

sad, _____ like the gen - tle

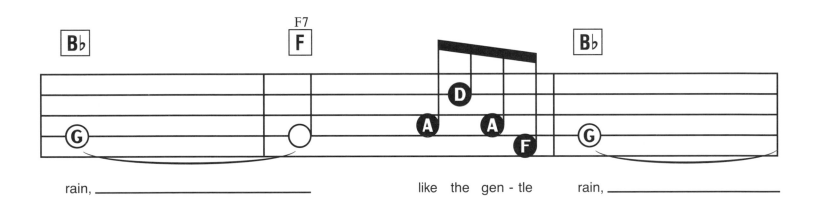

rain, _____ like the gen - tle rain, _____

_____ like the gen - tle rain. _____

Hello, Dolly!
from HELLO, DOLLY!

Registration 5
Rhythm: Swing

Music and Lyric by
Jerry Herman

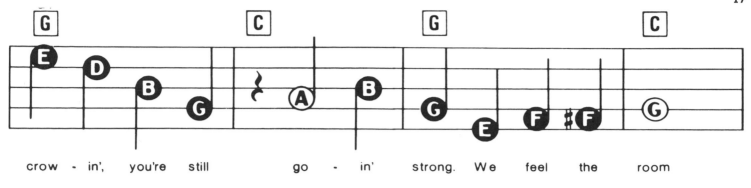

crow - in', you're still go - in' strong. We feel the room

sway - in', for the band's play - in' one of your old fa - v'rite

songs from 'way back when. So take her

wrap, fel - las, Find her an emp - ty lap, fel - las,

Dol - ly - 'll nev - er go a - way a - gain!_____

Hey, Look Me Over
from WILDCAT

Registration 7
Rhythm: 6/8 March

Music by Cy Coleman
Lyrics by Carolyn Leigh

Hey, look me o - ver, lend me an

ear; Fresh out of clo - ver, mort - gaged up to

here, _____ But don't pass the plate, folks, don't pass the

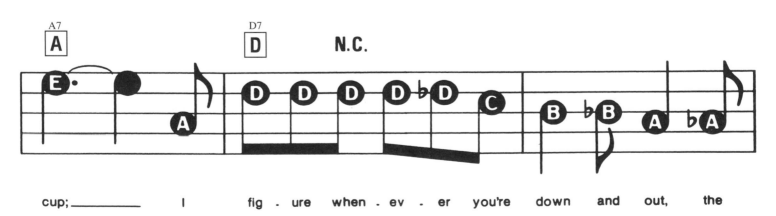

cup; _____ I fig - ure when - ev - er you're down and out, the

19

I Put a Spell on You

Registration 4
Rhythm: 6/8 Waltz

Words and Music by
Jay Hawkins

I put a spell on you, _____ (Instrumental)

be - cause _____ you're mine. _____

(Instrumental) You bet - ter

stop the thing _____ that you're do - ing. _____ I said - a

watch out, I ain't ly - in'. _____ Yeah! _____

I ain't gon - na take none of your fool - ing a - round. _____

I ain't gon - na take none of your put - ting me down. _____

_____ I put a spell on you, _____ (Instrumental)

be - cause _____ you're mine. ____ Whoa whoa,

22

al - right! (Instrumental)

I put a

Minnie the Moocher

Registration 2
Rhythm: Fox Trot or Swing

Words and Music by Cab Calloway
and Irving Mills

Hey, folks, here's a sto - ry of Min - nie the Mooch - er;
She messed a - round with a bloke ___ named Smok - ey.

she was a red hot hooch - ie cooch - er. She was the rough - est,
She loved ___ him, though he was a cok - ey. Now he took her down to

tough - est frail. Now, Min - nie had a heart as big as a whale. } Hi - de
Chi - na town and he showed her how to kick a gong ___ a - round. } Hi - de

hi - de hi - de hi. (Hi - de hi - de hi - de hi.) Ho - de ho - de ho - de ho. (Ho - de

24

Rhythm: Double-Time (♩=♩)

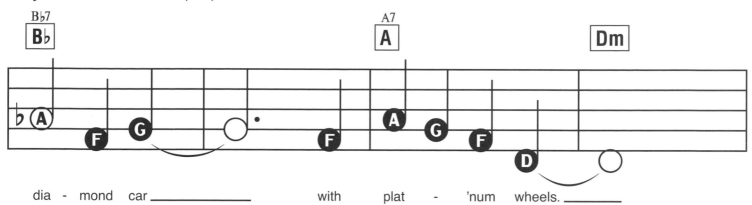

dia - mond car _____ with plat - 'num wheels. _____

Hi - de hi - de hi - de hi - de hi - de hi - de hi. (Hi - de hi - de hi - de hi - de

hi - de hi - de hi.) Ho - de ho - de ho - de ho - de ho - de ho - de ho.

(Ho - de ho - de ho - de ho - de ho - de ho - de ho.) He - de he - de he - de he - de

he - de he - de he. (He - de he - de he - de he - de he - de he - de he.)

Hi - de hi - de hi - de hi - de hi - de hi - de hi.

Rhythm: Tempo I

(Hi - de hi - de hi - de hi - de hi - de hi - de hi.) *(Instrumental)*

gave her his town-house and his rac - ing hors - es. Each meal she ate was a

doz - en cours - es. She had a mil - lion dol - lars in nick - els and dimes, she

sat a - round and count - ed one mil - lion times. Hi - de hi - de hi - de hi. (Hi - de

hi - de hi - de hi.) Ho - de ho - de ho - de ho. (Ho - de ho - de ho - de ho.) He - de

he - de he - de he. (He - de he - de he - de he.) Hi - de hi - de hi - de hi. (Hi - de

hi - de hi - de hi.) Poor Min, poor Min, poor Min.

I Shall Be Released

Registration 4
Rhythm: Country Rock or 8-Beat

Words and Music by
Bob Dylan

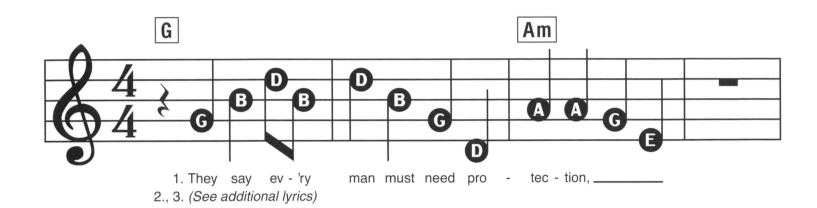

1. They say ev - 'ry man must need pro - tec - tion, _____
2., 3. *(See additional lyrics)*

they say ev - 'ry man must fall. _____

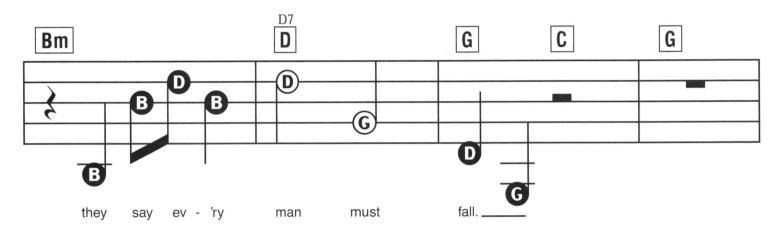

Yet I swear _____ I see my re - flec - tion _____

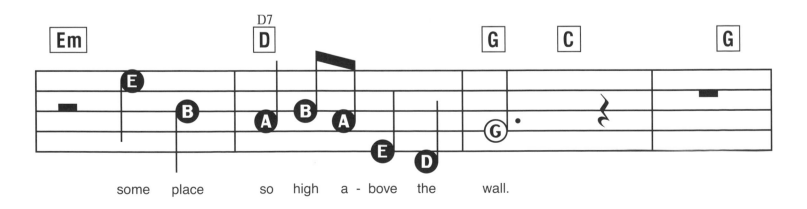

some place so high a - bove the wall.

Chorus

I see my light come shin - ing

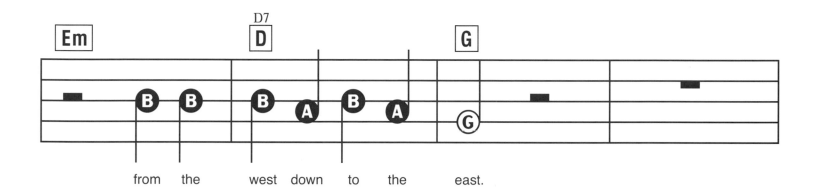

from the west down to the east.

An - y day now, an - y day now, I

shall be re - leased. leased.

Additional Lyrics

2. Down here next to me in this lonely crowd
Is a man who swears he's not to blame.
All day long I hear him cry so loud,
Calling out that he's been framed.
Chorus

3. They say ev'rything can be replaced,
Yet ev'ry distance is not near.
So I remember ev'ry face
Of ev'ry man who put me here.
Chorus

I Wanna Be Around

Registration 4
Rhythm: Swing or Jazz

Words by Johnny Mercer
Music by Sadie Vimmerstedt

I wan-na be a-round to pick up the piec-es, when some-bod-y breaks your

heart; Some some-bod-y twice as smart as I, _____

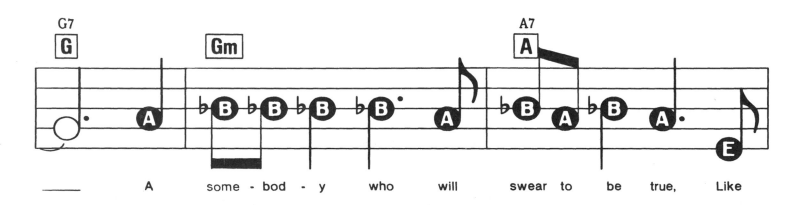

_____ A some-bod-y who will swear to be true, Like

you used to do with me. Who'll leave you to learn that

31

I'd Like to Teach the World to Sing

Registration 4
Rhythm: Rock

Words and Music by Bill Backer,
Roquel Davis, Roger Cook
and Roger Greenaway

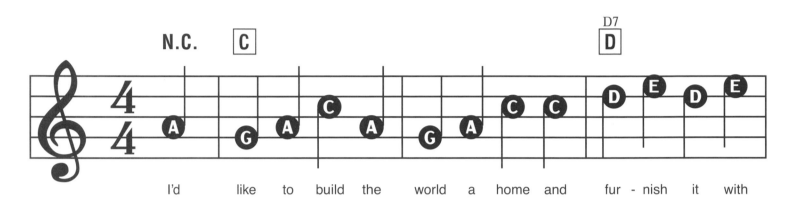

I'd like to build the world a home and fur - nish it with

love, grow ap - ple trees and hon - ey bees and snow - white tur - tle -

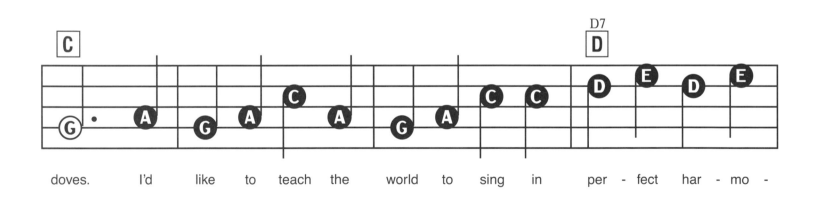

doves. I'd like to teach the world to sing in per - fect har - mo -

ny. I'd like to hold it in my arms and keep it com - pa -

33

I've Got a Gal in Kalamazoo

Registration 2
Rhythm: Swing or Jazz

Words by Mack Gordon
Music by Harry Warren

If I Had You

Registration 8
Rhythm: Fox Trot or Swing

Words and Music by Ted Shapiro,
Jimmy Campbell and Reg Connelly

Just You, Just Me

Registration 2
Rhythm: Swing or Fox Trot

Music by Jesse Greer
Lyrics by Raymond Klages

39

La Vie en Rose
(Take Me to Your Heart Again)

Registration 1
Rhythm: Fox Trot or Ballad

Original French Lyrics by Edith Piaf
Music by Luis Guglielmi
English Lyrics by Mack David

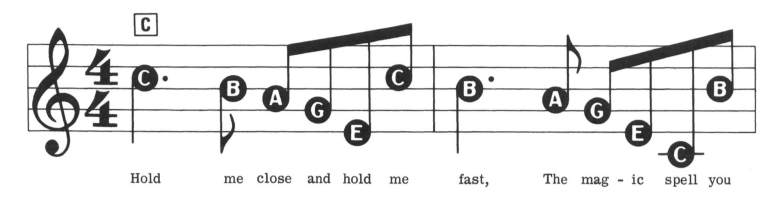

Hold me close and hold me fast, The mag-ic spell you

cast, This is la vie en rose._____ When you kiss me heav-en

sighs, And tho' I close my eyes I see la vie en rose._____

When you press me to your heart I'm in a world a-

41

part, A world where ros - es bloom; And when you speak an - gels

sing from a - bove; Ev - 'ry day words seem to

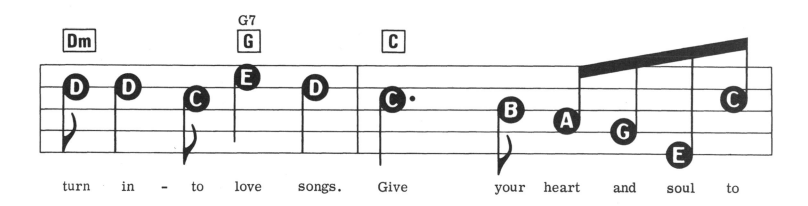

turn in - to love songs. Give your heart and soul to

me And life will al - ways be la vie en rose.

Laura

Registration 1
Rhythm: Fox Trot or 8-Beat

Lyrics by Johnny Mercer
Music by David Raksin

Lau - ra _____ is the face in the mist - y light, _____ foot - steps _____ that you hear down the hall. _____ The laugh _____ that floats on a sum - mer night, _____ that you can nev - er quite _____ re - call. _____

Mack the Knife
from THE THREEPENNY OPERA

English Words by Marc Blitzstein
Original German Words by Bert Brecht
Music by Kurt Weill

Registration 8
Rhythm: Swing

Mambo Italiano

Registration 7
Rhythm: Mambo or Latin

Words and Music by
Bob Merrill

Hey, mam - bo! Hey, Mam - bo I - tal - i - an - o!
Hey, mam - bo! Hey, Mam - bo I - tal - i - an - o!

Hey, mam - bo! Mam - bo I - tal - i - an - o! Go, go, go, you
Hey, mam - bo! Mam - bo I - tal - i - an - o! Bang bon - go and

mixed up Si - cil - i - an - o. All you Cal - a - braise - a do the
throw out the pic - co - lin - o. Shake - a, ba - by, shake - a 'cause I

mam - bo like a cra - zy with a Hey, mam - bo!
love - a when you take - a me to Hey, mam - bo!

47

Don't wan - na tar - an - tel - la; Hey mam - bo!
Down by the piz - zer - i - a, Ho, ho, ho,

No more - a moz - za - rel - la. Hey, mam - bo!
That's where I'm gon - na be - a. No, no, no,

Mam - bo I - tal - i - an - o! Try an en - chi - la - da with da
Don't tell - a ma - ma mi - a. Ma - ma say, "You stop - a or I'm

fish - a - bac - a - lah and then a Hey, goom - bah!
gon - na tell - a pa - pa." And a Hey, ja - drool,

48

Mr. Bojangles

Registration 3
Rhythm: Waltz

Words and Music by
Jerry Jeff Walker

(See Additional Lyrics)
2. I
3. He
4. He
5. He

Additional Lyrics

Verse 2 I met him in a cell in New Orleans
I was down and out.
He looked at me to be the eyes of age
As he spoke right out.
He talked of life, talked of life,
He laughed slapped his leg a step.
(Chorus)

Verse 3 He said his name, Bojangles,
Then he danced a lick across the cell.
He grabbed his pants a better stance
Oh, he jumped up high,
He clicked his heels.
He let go a laugh, let go a laugh,
Shook back his clothes all around
(Chorus)

Verse 4 He danced for those at minstrel shows
And county fairs throughout the South.
He spoke with tears of fifteen years
How his dog and he traveled about.
His dog up and died, he up and died,
After twenty years he still grieved.
(Chorus)

Verse 5 He said, "I dance now at every chance
In honky tonks for drinks and tips.
But most of the time I spend behind these county bars."
He said, "I drinks a bit."
He shook his head
And as he shook his head, I heard someone ask please
(Chorus)

Theme from "New York, New York"
from NEW YORK, NEW YORK

Registration 4
Rhythm: Swing

Words by Fred Ebb
Music by John Kander

54

55

king of the hill, head of the list, cream of the crop at the top of the heap.

My lit-tle town blues are melt-ing a-way.

I'll make a brand-new start of it in old New York.

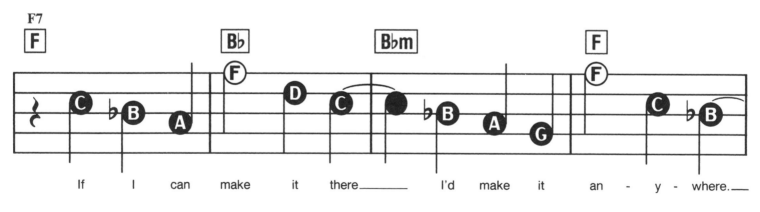

If I can make it there_____ I'd make it an-y-where.___

___ Come on, come through, New York, New York.___

On Broadway

Registration 1
Rhythm: Fox Trot

Words and Music by Barry Mann,
Cynthia Weil, Mike Stoller and Jerry Leiber

57

nough to eat / one thin dime / here gui - tar, The And glit one - ter I rubs thin right won't dime won't 'til

off and you're no - where on Broad - way. / e - ven shine your shoes on Broad way.

I'm a star on Broad - way. _____

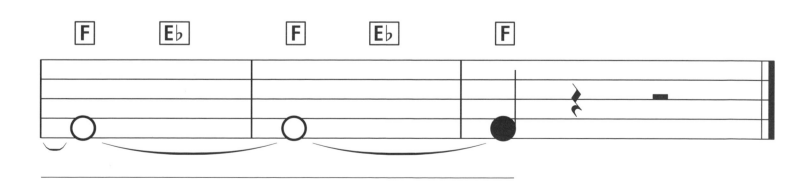

Over the Rainbow
from THE WIZARD OF OZ

Registration 5
Rhythm: Ballad

Music by Harold Arlen
Lyric by E.Y. "Yip" Harburg

dreams that you dare to dream real - ly do come true. Some -

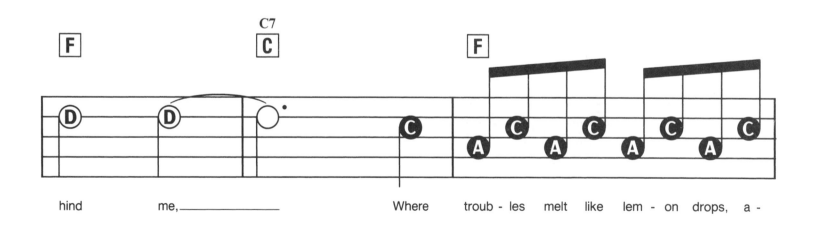

day I'll wish up - on a star and wake up where the clouds are far be -

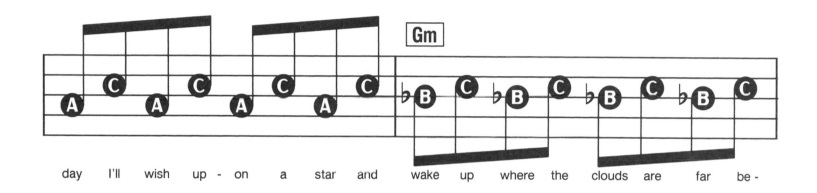

hind me,_____ Where troub - les melt like lem - on drops, a -

way, a - bove the chim - ney tops that's where you'll find me.

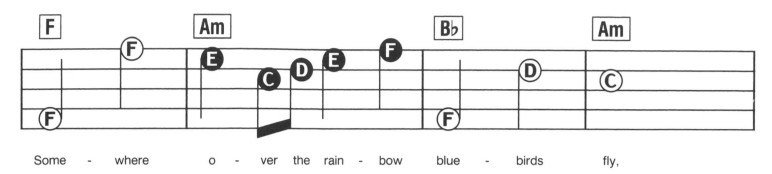

Some - where o - ver the rain - bow blue - birds fly,

Birds fly o - ver the rain - bow why then, oh why can't

I? I? If hap - py lit - tle blue - birds fly be -

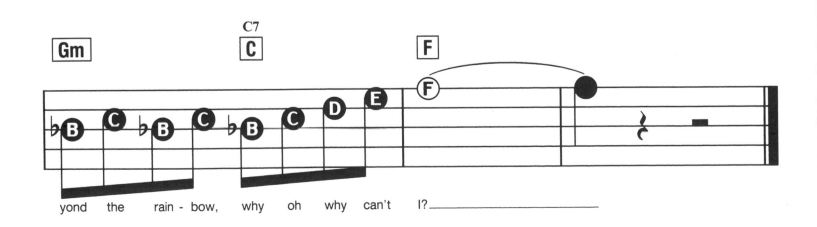

yond the rain - bow, why oh why can't I?_____

Pieces of Dreams
(Little Boy Lost)
from the Motion Picture PIECES OF DREAMS

Registration 8
Rhythm: Fox Trot or Swing

Lyrics by Alan and Marilyn Bergman
Music by Michel Legrand

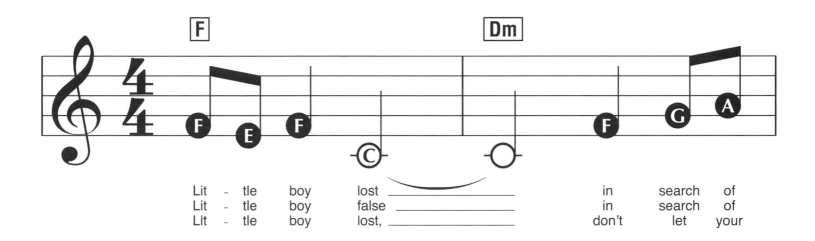

Lit - tle boy lost _____ in search of
Lit - tle boy false _____ in search of
Lit - tle boy lost, _____ don't let your

lit - tle boy found. _____ You go a -
lit - tle boy true. _____ Will you be
lit - tle sheep roam. _____ It's time, come

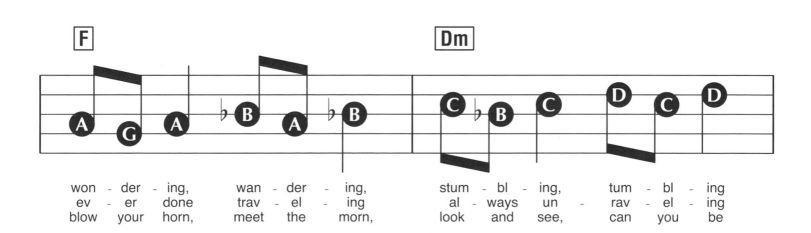

won - der - ing, wan - der - ing, stum - bl - ing, tum - bl - ing
ev - er done trav - el - ing al - ways un - rav - el - ing
blow your horn, meet the morn, look and see, can you be

63

September in the Rain

Registration 3
Rhythm: Ballad or Fox Trot

Words by Al Dubin
Music by Harry Warren

The Shadow of Your Smile
Love Theme from THE SANDPIPER

Registration 4
Rhythm: Bossa Nova or Latin

Music by Johnny Mandel
Words by Paul Francis Webster

The shad - ow of your smile when you are

gone _____ Will col - or all my dreams and light the

dawn. _____ Look in - to my eyes my love and

see _____ All the love - ly things you

Sing, Sing, Sing

Registration 4
Rhythm: Swing

Words and Music by
Louis Prima

Someone to Watch Over Me

Registration 7
Rhythm: Ballad or Swing

Music and Lyrics by George Gershwin
and Ira Gershwin

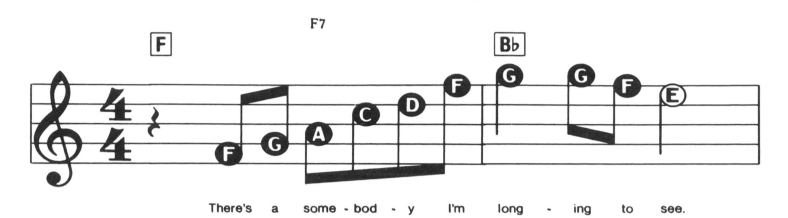

There's a some - bod - y I'm long - ing to see.

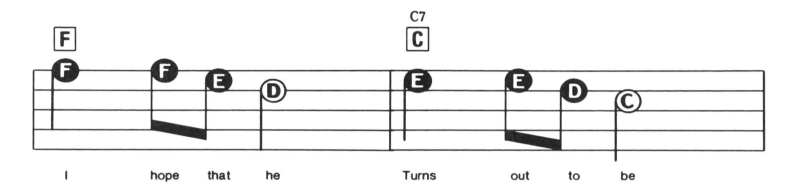

I hope that he Turns out to be

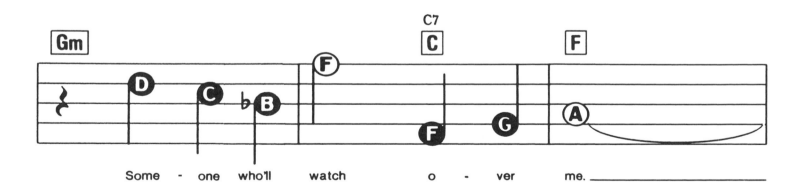

Some - one who'll watch o - ver me. _____

_____ I'm a lit - tle lamb who's

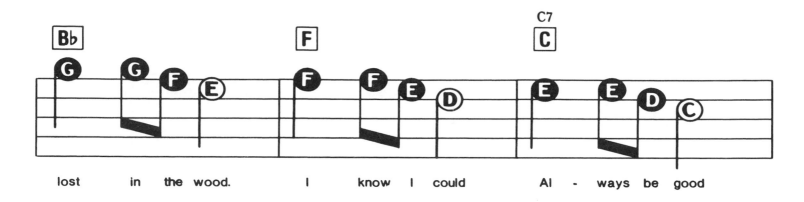

lost in the wood. I know I could Al - ways be good

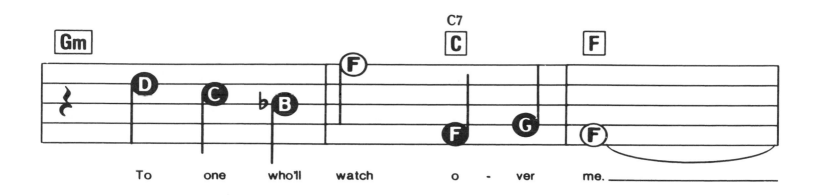

To one who'll watch o - ver me. _____

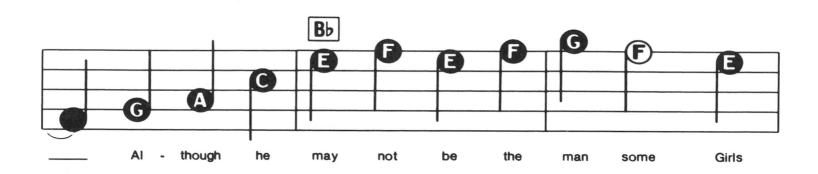

_____ Al - though he may not be the man some Girls

think of as hand - some. To my heart he

72

car - ries the key. _____

Won't you tell him please to put on some speed,

Fol - low my lead, Oh, how I need Some - one to

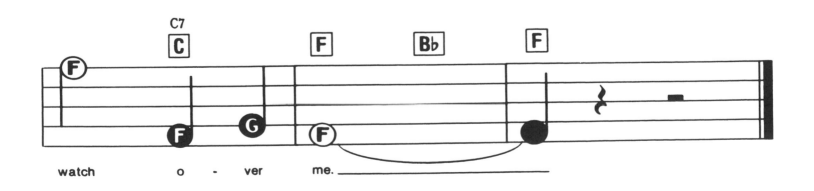

watch o - ver me. _____

Something's Gotta Give

Registration 5
Rhythm: Fox Trot or Swing

Words and Music by
Johnny Mercer

When an ir - re - sis - ti - ble force such as
When an ir - re - pres - si - ble smile such as
When an ir - re - sis - ti - ble force such as

you Meets an old _____ im - mov - a - ble
yours Warms an old _____ im - pla - ca - ble
you Meets an old _____ im - mov - a - ble

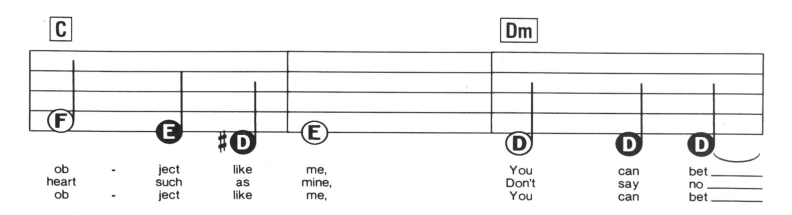

ob - ject like me, You can bet _____
heart such as me, mine, Don't say no _____
ob - ject like me, You can bet _____

To Coda ⊕

_____ as sure as you live, _____
_____ be - cause I in - sist _____
_____ as sure as you live, _____

sky? _____ I'll try hard _____

____ ig - nor - ing those lips I a - dore

But how long _____ can an - y - one try? _____

D.C. al Coda
(Return to beginning
Play to ⊕ and skip
to Coda)

Coda

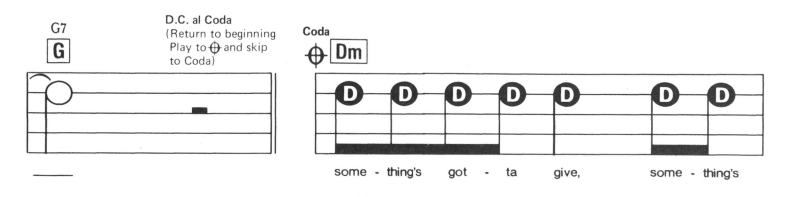

____ some - thing's got - ta give, some - thing's

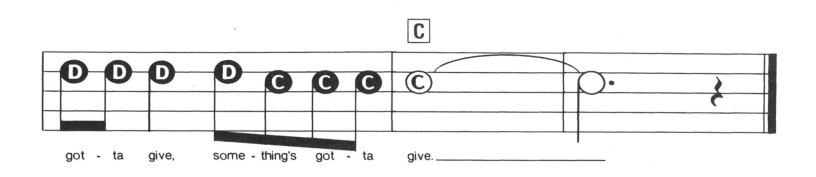

got - ta give, some - thing's got - ta give. _____

Stand by Your Man

Registration 3
Rhythm: Country or Shuffle

Words and Music by Tammy Wynette
and Billy Sherrill

Stars Fell on Alabama

Registration 1
Rhythm: Swing or Ballad

Words by Mitchell Parish
Music by Frank Perkins

Try a Little Tenderness

Registration 1
Rhythm: Swing or Ballad

Words and Music by Harry Woods,
Jimmy Campbell and Reg Connelly

82

word that's soft and gen - tle, Makes it eas - i - er to

bear. You won't re - gret it, Wom - en don't for - get it,

Love is their whole hap - pi - ness. It's all so eas - y;

try a lit - tle ten - der - ness._____

Song from M*A*S*H
(Suicide Is Painless)

Registration 5
Rhythm: Rock

Words and Music by Mike Altman
and Johnny Mandel

it if I please.

I

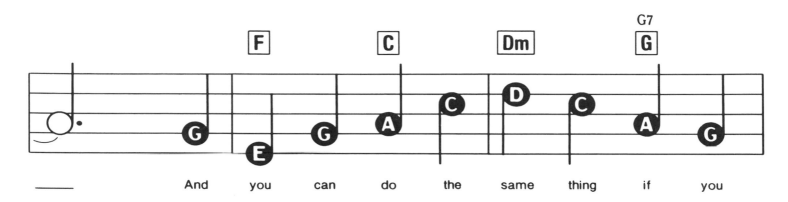

And you can do the same thing if you

please.

Additional Lyrics

2. I try to find a way to make
 All our little joys relate
 Without that ever present hate
 But now I know that it's too late.
 And *Chorus*

3. The game of life is hard to play,
 I'm going to lose it anyway,
 The losing card I'll someday lay
 So this is all I have to say;
 That *Chorus*

4. The only way to win, is cheat
 And lay it down before I'm beat,
 And to another give a seat
 For that's the only painless feat.
 'Cause *Chorus*

5. The sword of time will pierce our skins,
 It doesn't hurt when it begins,
 But as it works its way on in,
 The pain grows stronger, watch it grin.
 For *Chorus*

6. A brave man once requested me
 To answer questions that are key,
 Is it to be or not to be
 And I replied; "Oh, why ask me."
 'Cause *Chorus*

Summer Wind

Registration 7
Rhythm: Swing

English Words by Johnny Mercer
Original German Lyrics by Hans Bradtke
Music by Henry Mayer

The sum - mer wind came blow - ing in a -

cross the sea,_____ It lin-gered there to touch your hair and

walk with me._____ All sum-mer long we sang a song and

strolled the gold - en sand, Two sweet-hearts and the

Sweet Georgia Brown

Registration 7
Rhythm: Fox Trot or Swing

Words and Music by Ben Bernie,
Maceo Pinkard and Kenneth Casey

No gal made has got a shade on sweet Geor - gia Brown,

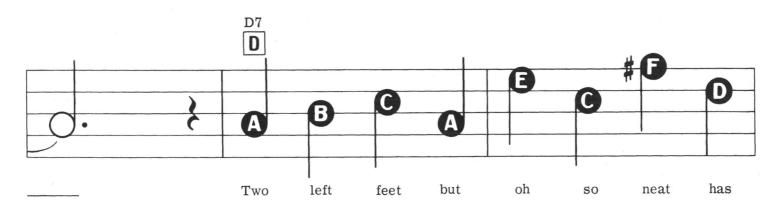

Two left feet but oh so neat has

sweet Geor - gia Brown;_____ They all sigh and

wan - na die for sweet Geor-gia Brown,_____ I'll tell___ you just why,_____

Tea for Two

Registration 8
Rhythm: Shuffle or Swing

Words by Irving Caesar
Music by Vincent Youmans

Tender Is the Night

Registration 1
Rhythm: Swing or Ballad

Words by Paul Francis Webster
Music by Sammy Fain

Ten - der is the night, so ten - der is the night. There's

no one in the world ex - cept the two of us._____

Should to - mor - row find us dis - en - chant - ed,_____

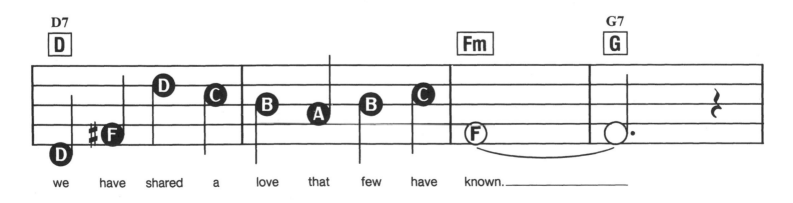

we have shared a love that few have known._____

The Trolley Song
from MEET ME IN ST. LOUIS

Registration 4
Rhythm: Swing

Words and Music by Hugh Martin
and Ralph Blane

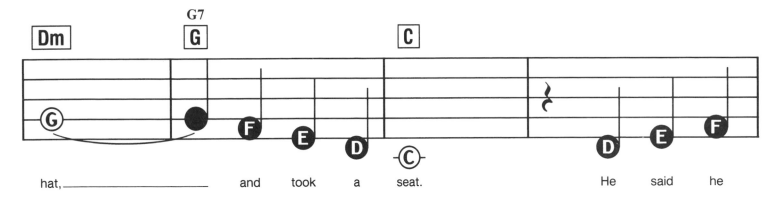

hat,_____ and took a seat. He said he

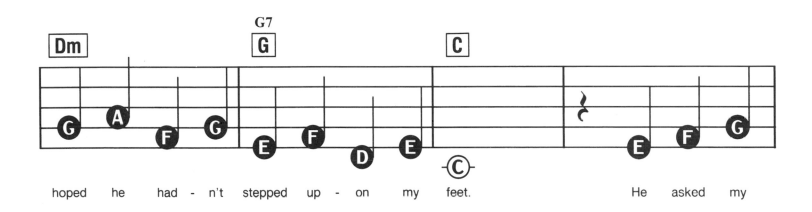

hoped he had - n't stepped up - on my feet. He asked my

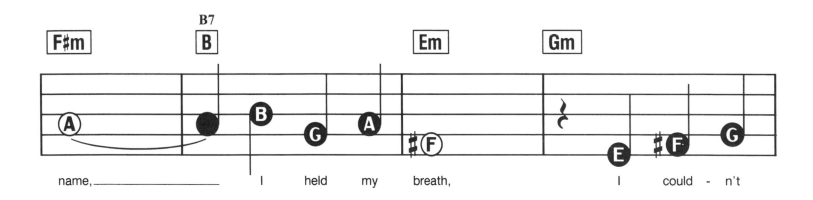

name,_____ I held my breath, I could - n't

D.C. al Fine
(Return to beginning
Play to Fine)

speak be - cause he scared me half to death._____

What Is This Thing Called Love?

Registration 7
Rhythm: Fox Trot or Swing

Words and Music by
Cole Porter

What is this thing _____ called

love? This fun - ny thing _____ called

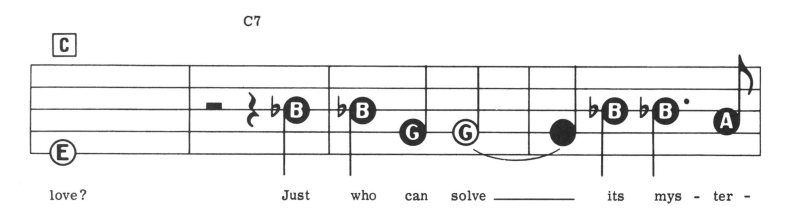

love? Just who can solve _____ its mys - ter -

y? Why should it make _____ a fool of

97

The Wind Beneath My Wings

Registration 3
Rhythm: Rock

Words and Music by Larry Henley
and Jeff Silbar

99

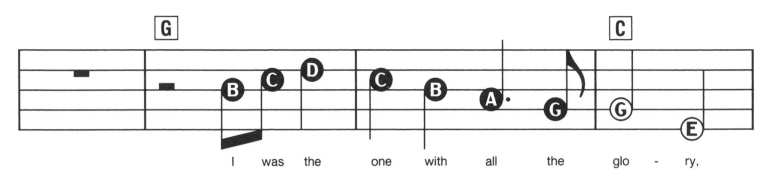

I was the one with all the glo - ry,

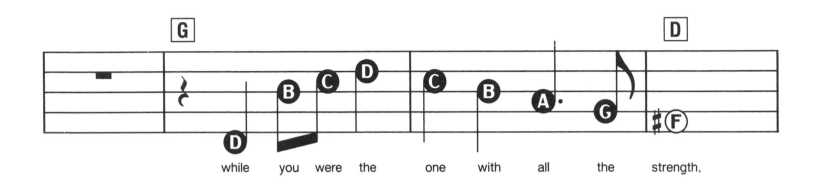

while you were the one with all the strength,

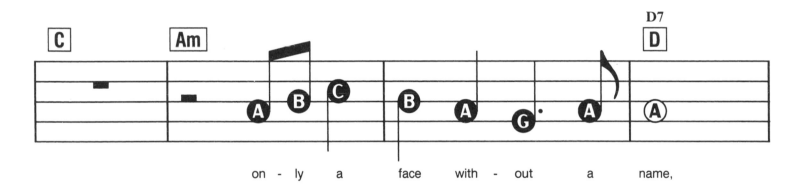

on - ly a face with - out a name,

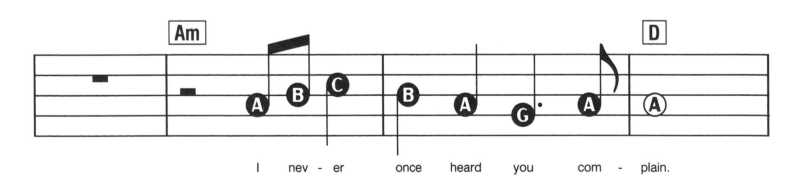

I nev - er once heard you com - plain.

Did you ev - er know that you're my_____

he - ro, and ev - 'ry - thing I'd like to

be? I can fly high - er than an

ea - gle, _____ 'cause you are the

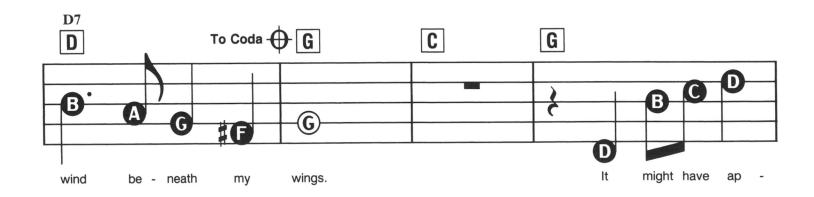

wind be - neath my wings. It might have ap -

peared to go un - no - ticed that I've got it

all here in my heart. I want you to

know I know the truth: I would be

D.S. al Coda
(Return to 𝄋
Play to ⨁ and
skip to Coda)

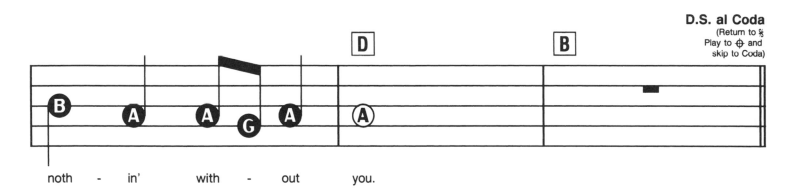

noth - in' with - out you.

CODA

wings. You are the

wind be - neath my_____ wings.

What You Won't Do for Love

Registration 1
Rhythm: Funk or Rock

Words and Music by Bobby Caldwell
and Alfons Kettner

103